secret
ASIAN
man

*For Pauline
Many thanks
and in
admiration for your
poems.*

by
Nick
Carbó

*Nick
Carbó*

Tia Chucha Press, Chicago

Acknowledgments

The author would like to thank the editors of the following publications in which these poems first appeared.

Asian Pacific American Journal: Ang Tunay na Lalaki Visits his Favorite Painting; Ang Tunay na Lalaki is Baffled by Cryptic Messages; Ang Tunay na Lalaki Lies Nude on the Bed; Ang Tunay na Lalaki Considers the Historical Consequences. *Barrow Street:* Ang Tunay na Lalaki Meets Barbie at the Shark Bar. *Crab Orchard Review:* Ang Tunay na Lalaki's Friend Shows up Unannounced. *Flippin': Filipinos on America:* Ang Tunay na Lalaki Stalks the Streets of New York. *Hayden's Ferry Review:* Ang Tunay na Lalaki is Addicted to New York. *Likhaan, UP Creative Writing Center's Online Magazine:* Ang Tunay na Lalaki Goes Back in Time to 1888. *Luna:* Secret Asian Man. *Plaeidies:* Ang Tunay na Lalaki Does his Laundry. *Phatitude:* Ang Tunay na Lalaki Tries to Explain to his Therapist. *Sundog:* Aswang vs Wonder Woman. *Tilting the Continent: Southeast Asian American Literature:* Ang Tunay na Lalaki Receives a Package fom Home. *Urbanus:* Ang Tunay na Lalaki Writes his Dream Dictionary.

The author gratefully acknowledges residencies at the MacDowell Colony, Fundacíon Valparaíso (Spain), and Le Chateau de Lavigny/Ledig Rowohlt Foundation (Switzerland), and fellowships in poetry from the National Endowment for the Arts in 1997 and the New York Foundation for the Arts in 1999 which were instrumental in the support of this book. Thanks to the following individuals: Maureen Seaton and Eric Gamalinda for the kind words, Luis J. Rodriguez, Jean Valentine, Jane Cooper, E. San Juan, Jr., Regie Cabico, Stephanie Strickland, Eileen Tabios, Allison Joseph, Barbara Ess, Oliver de la Paz, Ron Drummond, Luis H. Francia, Peter Drizal, Thomas E. Kennedy, Robert Hass, Steven Styers, Lisa Glatt, Kevin Prufer, Eugene Gloria, Jimmy Abad, NVM Gonzalez, Fatima Lim-Wilson, Luisa Igloria, Krip Yuson, Patrick Pardo, Naomi Shihab-Nye, John Wheatcroft, Karl Patten, and Molly Peacock for all the encouragement. And many thanks to my parents Alfonso & Sophie and to my ever beautiful wife Denise.

Printed in the United States of America.

Library of Congress Catalog Card Number: 00-130213.

Book Design: Jane Brunette
Cover Art: Nancy Lanctot
Back Cover Photo: Ann Burrola

Published by:
Tia Chucha Press
A Project of the Guild Complex
PO Box 476969
Chicago IL 60647

Distributed by:
Northwestern University Press
Chicago Distribution Center
11030 South Langley Avenue
Chicago IL 60628

Tia Chucha Press and Guild Complex have received support from the John D. and Catherine T. MacArthur Foundation, Lannan Foundation, Sara Lee Foundation, National Endowment for the Arts, the Illinois Arts Council, Kraft Foods, City of Chicago Department of Cultural Affairs, Lila Wallace-Readers Digest Fund, Eric Mathieu King Fund of the Academy of American Poets, The Chicago Community Foundation, the Reva and David Logan Foundation, the Illinois Humanities Council, Poets & Writers, The Woods Fund of Chicago, WPWR-TV Channel 50 Foundation, The Mayer and Morris Kaplan Family Foundation, Driehaus Foundation, and the Elizabeth F. Cheney Foundation.

This book is dedicated to the memory of
Joseph Illeto,
Filipino American postman shot nine times
on August 10, 1999 in Los Angeles, California
by a white supremacist.

Contents

Part 4

Part 5

Part One

∎∎∎

Ang Tunay na Lalalaki means
"The Real Man" in Tagalog.
He was a bare-chested muscled Filipino
male character in television commercials in the Philippines
during the 70's and 80's that advertised
a local brand of hard liquor.
Ang Tunay na Lalaki's American counterparts
are the Marlboro Man and Mr. Clean.

■ ■ ■

ANG TUNAY NA LALAKI
STALKS THE STREETS OF NEW YORK

looking to harvest what makes him happy.
The AA meetings have thrown
him into sacrilegious jousts with Titans

and Gorgons with glowing snake eyes
and leather pants. This is life
without the Filipino bottle,

without the star fruit boogie,
without the *bomba* films. He wears black
Dr. Martens boots because slippers

would expose his *provinciano* feet
to the snow. He wants to ride
the back of a *carabao* and bolt

up Madison Avenue screaming
like Tandang Sora or shout
hala-bira! hala-bira! hala-bira!

like his Isneg cousins in Aklan.
Ay, susmaryosep! Such bad behavior
from the "true male" of Filipino

advertising. He looks at his reflection
on a book store window, notices
that his hair has grown shoulder-length—

like Tonto in the Lone Ranger
he would watch on TV. He turns to the right,
his profile now looks like the young Bruce Lee

9

as Kato in the Green Hornet. Yes,
he realizes it will always be the face
of a supporting character. Rejected

from the Absolut Vodka ads, he decides
to change his name for an upcoming audition
for a Preparation H commercial—Al Moranas,

American but with a Filipino flare.

■ ■ ■
ANG TUNAY NA LALAKI
IS BAFFLED BY CRYPTIC MESSAGES

he finds on cheap match covers.

> PLEASE
> MAKE ME TASTE LIKE
> A MAN

is the first one he reads after lighting up
an American Spirit cigarette on the corner
of Broadway and Houston. The painted Statue

of Liberty on the giant DKNY ad on the side
of the building winks her big blue eye
as if she understands what those words mean,

as if she could make him taste like a man.
The street sign changes to WALK
and the natural smoke of the natural cigarette

feels good in his lungs. He thinks
of the taste of fried garlic, of anise seeds,
of rambutan fruit, of broiled tuna—

none comes close to what a man
would taste like in his mind. He reaches
underneath his shirt and sweater to scratch

his left armpit. He smells his fingers
and thinks, this is what a Filipino man
must taste like to American women.

To test his hypothesis, he sticks
his index finger in his mouth, pulls
it out with a slurpy sound and points upwards

as if he were testing the wind,
as if he were about to satisfy a desire,
as if he were carrying a flaming torch.

■ ■ ■

ANG TUNAY NA LALAKI
VISITS HIS FAVORITE PAINTING

in the Metropolitan Museum of Art. Not
the Renoirs, the Picassos, the Van Goghs,
or the Titians—he is attracted to a watercolor

by an American, Winslow Homer's
Palm Tree, 1898. The scene is Nassau
but it could well be Cavite, Nasugbu, or Boracay

back home. The aquamarine blue
is truly tropical where one could dive in
and read the *New York Times*, watch

the lobsters and the parrot fish
look over the classifieds, or observe
a puffer fish inflate over an article

about the depletion of the rain forests.
The wind blows from right to left
in the foreground and the strips

of palm leaves agree. He can hear
the wind's missives translated
by the leaves—

barometric pressure dropping,
mostly cloudy with cumulus clouds,
something big in the air.

The red flag by the white
lighthouse in the background
blows from left to right suggesting

a circular wind. He remembers
the same conditions on Boracay island
when he looked up and saw the clear

over-heated eye of an angry typhoon.

■ ■ ■

ANG TUNAY NA LALAKI
GOES BACK IN TIME TO MAY 1888

when Jose Rizal was in New York City
to board a ship to London and Spain.
The streets smell bad
because of the horses and mules moving
everyone around. Grover Cleveland is at the end
of his first term as President and most
of the New York avenues are lighted by electricity.

He is lost in this part of time and does not know
where to look for Rizal. He sneaks
into the Metropolitan Opera House
where they're performing Tchaikovsky's new
Swan Lake but he can't spot a brown face
in the crowd with his opera glasses. He takes
the no. 4 steam street car to the Brooklyn Bridge,
walks to the apex of the span
and shouts *Rizal! Rizal! Donde estás!*
Only the grey-blue seagulls answer him.
Dejected, he walks towards Battery Park.

He feels a stone slam into his back and hears
look, a dirty savage Indian! Let's get 'im!
White teenaged boys swarm towards him
and he has nowhere to go except over the rocks
into the Hudson River. Out of reach
of their projectiles, he continues swimming
further into the current. Up ahead
the newly dedicated Statue of Liberty is growing
bigger and closer and bigger
and he feels tired, hungry, and poor.

■ ■ ■

ANG TUNAY NA LALAKI
IS ADDICTED TO NEW YORK

fantasy phone sex
and he swims
the voodoo

of her voice
@ $4.99/minute,
asking her to repeat

"I am a possessed witch."
Her name is Anne
and she blows

smoke on his thighs
as he slumps himself
on his easy chair.

She gives good
similes and his penis
is as big as Brazil,

as warm as an incandescent
light bulb, as hard
as Muhammad Ali's jaw.

She tantalizes him
with fancy words like
tristesse, ennui, juxtapose,

cicatrix, and hyperbole.
With each savory syllable,
her tongue trochees

from the base
to the top of his penis,
spondees around the head.

Part
Two
...

■ ■ ■

ANG TUNAY NA LALAKI
DOES HIS LAUNDRY

at the Liquid Sky
on Lafayette between Prince
and Spring Streets because
he likes the name, because
he liked Melanie Griffith in the movie,
because *Esquire Magazine* listed
laundromats as a top-ten place
to meet single women. He presses
his face against the glass
where a curtain of water cascades
down the other side of the window.
No aliens stealing orgasms,
no skinny women in Calvin Klein thongs,
not even old ladies with pet Chihuahuas.
As he watches his three weeks worth
of clothes circle inside the mega-loader,
he slips into a heroin-like trance—
he drifts within an Amorsolo painting,
the one with brightly clad women
washing clothes on the banks of a river.
Back home his maid did the laundry,
called a "lavandera," a washer woman
who washed all day
on the banks of a river.
There's no other sound like clothes
slapped against a rock
on the banks of a river—
thap, thap, thap, thap, thap, thap,
on the banks of a river.
A guy with Apollonian eyes
wearing short blue running shorts

has his hand on his knee, saying
he's unbalanced, no, his load is
unbalanced, thap, thap, thap,
in the mega-loader.

■ *for Gerald Slota*

■ ■ ■

ANG TUNAY NA LALAKI
SIPS A FROTHY CAPPUCCINO

at Cafe Gitanes on Mott and Prince
and the guy with Apollonian eyes
asks if the seat next to him
is occupied. He says his name
is Orpheus, originally from Greece
and he asks Ang Tunay na Lalaki
if he's from the Philippines.
"How did you guess that," he responds,
putting down his mug. Orpheus cracks
a smile, "I've recently traveled
to Manila through a poem
by a poet named Nick Carbó.
I was made to levitate over cars,
meet Filipino mythological figures,
go to bars where the waiters were dwarves,
and visit restaurants where you eat
with your hands and fingers."
Ang Tunay na Lalaki takes a drag
from his cigarette, "Wow! That must be
a great life, going all over the world,
living the thoughts of some poet.
I've always feared that was happening
to me, that I was someone's figment
just like in Calderon de la Barca's
La Vida es Sueño."
Orpheus places his hand on
Ang Tunay na Lalaki's knee, "Trust me,
it's not that great. Poets
are hardly faithful to you,
they drop you as soon as they finish
the poem. Poets can also be cruel—

living out their little evil fantasies
through your body."
Ang Tunay na Lalaki crosses
his legs, "Yeah, I know what you mean.
I once had the urge to ride
a *Carabao* up Madison Avenue
and run down all the people
with designer shopping bags. Strange,
everything I do seems to happen
in the third person." Orpheus grabs
Ang Tunay na Lalaki's arm, whispers,
"Maybe we're both characters
in somebody's love-starved poem
and I'm here to seduce you."
Orpheus looks up
through the nicotine haze
and addresses the ceiling.
Well, I spilled the beans.
I know what you're up to.
Ang Tunay na Lalaki coughs
into the cappuccino, pours
some on his lap. "I have to go,
I'm late for my therapist."
Ang Tunay na Lalaki's strides
quicken as he nears Houston
and Mott. *I should have guessed*
with a name like Orpheus he'd be
a nut case. All that stuff
about being a character in a poem—
Hah! Get a life! And who is
this Nick Carbó poet anyway?
Never heard of him.

■ ■ ■
ANG TUNAY NA LALAKI'S
FRIEND SHOWS UP UNANNOUNCED

one afternoon with a purple suitcase.
They both started out
in the Filipino commercials
about the same time and both men
were popular with women. However,
Charlie Balakubak was condemned
to use a special shampoo to control
his dandruff which, when not applied daily,
caused a trail of flakes that even Hansel and Gretel
would find easy to follow through the darkest
of forests. *"Kumusta! Pare, long time*
no see, at, hoy, you're pogi as eber."
Ang Tunay na Lalaki grins, "How
did you find me? And what's with that big
purple suitcase?" Charlie's smile drops,
"Hoy, pare. Aren't you glad to see
your blood brother? So, now that you hab
that American accent, you don't hab time
por your Pilipino prends. *Ang bigat, heby, conio*
naman kayo!" Ang Tunay na Lalaki lifts
the purple suitcase and heads inside the building.
"O.K., but no long term stay. Are you vacationing
or going to look for a job in New York?"
Charlie follows timidly, "Don't you remember
the good times we had? All those nights
in the discos, swimming nude in Boracay,
all the women we shared—remember
when I got the Palm Olive girl and you had
the Camay soap beauty and we switched
and they smelled so good even after
you were sweating on their breasts?

Sige *naman*, what happened to you,
you're so *pinche?*" "Sixth floor
walk up," Ang Tunay na Lalaki warns,
"And I'm living the American dream."
Charlie's eyes widen, "*Ano*, you hab
American girlprend? Groovy, man.
Totally awesome inside the wave, cool!
Is she like Farah Fawcett with big hair,
like Darryl Hannah, like Julia Roberts?
I know *ang* type *mo*, she's probably
a Vogue model, *hindi ba?*"
Ang Tunay na Lalaki drops
the suitcase beside his blue futon couch,
"Have a seat. And *walang akong* girlprend—
It's *girl-fffffff-friend*. Get that straight,
f is not pronounced as *p* and *have* has no *b*
in it! Speak English!" Charlie wipes
beads of sweat from his brow, "*Ano, ba?*
You don't want to share your *fffffucking*
girl-fffffriend? How's that English por you!"
Ang Tunay na Lalaki takes two beers
from his fridge, "That's better
but you need to practice. *Fffffor*, not *por*.
You'll never pass an audition in New York
until you improve your accent and learn
how to sing like Lea Salonga in Miss Saigon.
Did you bring your Chinese dresses?"
"*Talaga?* I have to wear dresses
to get a part in a production?" he asks,
fanning himself with a magazine.
"Name the top ten male leads in Hollywood
and how many Asian hunks have you seen
involved in hot sex scenes with a Sharon Stone,
Demi Moore, or Goldie Hawn?" Ang Tunay
na Lalaki sits next to Charlie and grabs
his crotch, "We have no balls, no penis,
no nothing in this country."

■ ■ ■

ANG TUNAY NA LALAKI
EXPLORES THE CHAT ROOMS ON AOL

You have entered room: Town Square
"The tendency of statistical averages
69TNGHT: Any chicks here?
to remain stable if the conditions remain
Buggy: and they took the car to NJ
stable is one of the most remarkable
       to Sarah's house
characteristics of our universe.
MacMoth: 16/F here.
It can be explained, I hold, only
69TNGHT: Hi, MacMoth. 17/M in LA.
by the propensity theory; by the theory
You have entered room: WM4Couples
that there exists weighted possibilities
Ty565: and his schlong was huge, like a house
that are more than near possibilities, but tendencies
       colonial, with Doric columns.
or propensities to become real: tendencies
Lalaki: Hello room. Hi from the Big Apple.
or propensities to realize themselves that are
Ty565: I painted that house with my tongue.
inherent in all possibilities in varying degrees
Concord2: Anybody for some cyber?
and which are something like forces that keep
You have entered room: submissive m4F
the statistics stable. Propensities, it is assumed,
MisPain: don't forget to lick between my toes.
are not mere possibilities but are physical
HAT80: Yes, mistress P. Tastes so good.
realities. They are as real as forces, or fields
       May I proceed to your ankle?

of forces. And vice versa: forces are propensities.
MisPain: First, suck each toe
They are propensities for setting bodies in motion.
like you mean it, slave!
Forces are propensities to accelerate, and fields
You make me so hard!
of forces are propensities distributed over
MisPain: Did I say you can get a boner?
some region of space and perhaps changing
(slaps HAT80's butt, repeatedly)
continuously over this region (like distances
HAT80: Thank you Mistress. I deserve it.
from some given origin). Fields of forces are
(buttocks red, stinging, penis shrinking)
fields of propensities; they are real, they exist.
MisPain: That's better, you cock sucking
Propensities, like Newtonian attractive forces,
pathetic piece of celery.
are invisible, and, like them, they can act:
You may now kiss the insides
they are actual, they are real. We therefore are
of my thighs. Slave! Slowly!
compelled to attribute a kind of reality to mere
HAT80: Yes, Mistress, I'm here to please you.
possibilities, especially to weighted possibilities…
(Chimes): INSTANT MESSAGE
This view of propensities allows us to see
ClaraB: Hello, Lalaki.
in a new light the processes that constitute
Respond?
our world: the world process. The world
Lalaki: Hi
is no longer a CAUSAL MACHINE—it can
ClaraB: I like your profile. Are you Hawaiian?
now be seen as a world of propensities, as
Lalaki: No, Filipino. N U?

an unfolding process of realizing possibilities
ClaraB: Mongrel American. Are you a SUB?
and of unfolding possibilities.
Lalaki: No. Only good manners which can be
In all these cases the propensity theory allows
      mistaken for submissive behavior.
us to work with an objective theory
ClaraB: LOL :)
of probability. Quite apart from the fact
ClaraB: What do you do?
that we do not know the future, the future
Lalaki: Actor in NY, but carpenter by day.
is objectively not fixed. The future is open:
      N U?
objectively open. Only the past is fixed; it
ClaraB: Married housewife. Mistress at night.
has been actualized and so it is gone.
Lalaki: Does HE know you do this?
The PRESENT can be described as the
ClaraB: My husband's a lawyer, away most
continuing process of the actualization
      of the time. He doesn't know.
of propensities." -Karl Popper
Lalaki: Is he submissive?
Lalaki: Are you there?
Lalaki: Hello?
Lalaki: Are you there?
Lalaki: Hello?
(ClaraB is no longer available to receive messages)

■ *for Pelle Lowe*

■ ■ ■

ANG TUNAY NA LALAKI
MEETS BARBIE AT THE SHARK BAR

on Mulberry and Spring on a rainy night.
Her head sticks out of some woman's tote bag
placed on top of the bar, she winks
at Ang Tunay na Lalaki. He looks at his gin and tonic,
looks back at the doll and hears her tiny voice
even though her lips aren't moving. "Hi there,
big guy. I was made in the Philippines. You look
like you were made there too." He responds
just to humor himself, "Where, at the Subic Bay
manufacturing plants? Did you enjoy
being made by exploited laborers?" Barbie crawls
onto the sticky bar and sits herself on the edge
crossing her legs. "I remember those delicate fingers
expertly sewing the hairs to my head. Those women
were so nice to me." She bends at her waist
to let her hair down and dramatically lifts her head up
so her blond locks turn into a glamorous puff,
"See, they did a good job. You must admit."
"You're incorrigible," he exhales a cloud of smoke
after lighting up a cigarette, "And you're
all plastic, petroleum based plastic."
Barbie places her palms against her face
and begins to sob. Ang Tunay na Lalaki sticks out
his middle finger, strokes the back of her head,
"Now, now, doll. First time anyone ever told
you the truth?" Barbie lifts her left arm
to swipe away his finger, "My name's Barbie!
Not Doll, Sweetie, Honey, or Dolly. It's Barbie!"
Ang Tunay na Lalaki sips his gin,
"Look, Barbie. You have the perfect life,
you're the world's best-selling doll

and millions of little girls are buying you dresses.
Even the top fashion designers design
outfits for you." Barbie straightens her back
as if she had a spine, places
her hands on her lap, "But you don't know
how hard it is to be beautiful all the time. See,
you made my mascara run." He takes a napkin,
dips it into his drink, proceeds to wipe off
the small black streaks on her cheeks, "It's acrylic,
a water based paint." He reaches into his pocket
for a ball-point pen, draws rich eye lashes
around her eyes. Barbie slides over to a shot glass,
stares at her reflection, "Hey, you're good
at this. Have you ever considered a career
in make-up? I could recommend you
to our designers, you know."
Suddenly a woman's human hand plucks
Barbie off the bar, stuffing her
back into a tote bag. His eyes follow
the tote bag out the door. All he can see
is a puff of blond hair and a stiff arm
swaying back and forth like a metronome.

■ *for Denise*

■ ■ ■
ANG TUNAY NA LALAKI
RECEIVES A PACKAGE FROM HOME

and out of the layers of newspapers pops up
the wooden statue of La Virgen del Pelo Mojado.
The note attached to her feet is from his mother
reminding him, *"Querido hijo,* the reason
why you may have not yet found a wife
is that you don't go to church. This is a replica
of our town's miraculous Virgin. She will help you.
Pray to her, *hijo.* The wife will come."
Ang Tunay na Lalaki is sure his mother has arranged
for a novena for the next six months at their church.
He can't bare to think of the whole town including
him in their prayers— "Please Holy Mother, help
Lalakito find a good American wife."

The next day, he notices all sorts of women smiling
at him on the streets of New York. An auburn-haired
woman with a French accent asks him directions
to the Armani Exchange store. An Indian woman
in a sari asks him for the time. Even a group
of parfum-scented Filipinas stop him on Mercer
looking for the swanky Cendrillon restaurant.
On the N train, he hands a couple of quarters
to a homeless woman who says, *"Que Dios
te bendiga. Tu mujer te esta esperando."*
Your woman is waiting for you. The train swerves,
he grabs a pole to steady himself. He looks
for the homeless woman but she's gone.
He wants to know *where* she's waiting for him.

Back at his apartment he finds no fancy looking letters
in his mail box, no messages on his answering machine.

He takes La Virgen del Pelo Mojado from the floor,
places her on the mantle piece, and begins
to arrange the flowers he bought into two high
water glasses which he will place on both sides
of his miraculous Virgin of the Wet Hair.

Part
Three
...

■ ■ ■

ANG TUNAY NA LALAKI
DECIDES TO CATCH A GODDARD FILM

at the Angelika Theaters on Houston and Mercer.
He takes an aisle seat in the third row
because he likes being near the action and tall people
usually don't like craning their necks upwards
with the screen so close. Well, at least
that's his theater seat theory. Just as the previews
get rolling, a woman with her tall date stand
near him. "No, no, this one. That's too close,"
says the date. The woman excuses herself
to get into his row, spilling half her popcorn
on his parted legs and onto his seat because his butt
is up against the back of his chair to let them in. Her long
black wet hair smacks against Ang Tunay na Lalaki's face
as she turns to apologize, swiping popcorn from his legs.
"Shit! Just sit down, Sally," the tall date mutters.
The movie begins and he feels a few grains
of salt under his legs. "Damn it, Sally!
You didn't say this was going to be in French
and in subtitles. I didn't bring my glasses," utters
the tall date. Ten minutes into the film he says,
"This is so bad. Nothing's happening. Let's go
back to my place." The woman hushes him.
Twelve minutes and the tall date ejaculates,
"This is elitist crap! Come on, let's get
our money back. I'm leaving!" The woman stays
transfixed by the screen, says one word, "Go."
Ang Tunay na Lalaki gets up to let the tall date out
and hears him cursing, "Artsy-fartsy bitch."
The woman with wet hair doesn't say a word,
even through the ending credits of the film.
He starts to get up after the music dies

and he hears her ask, "I just love Jean-Luc.
Don't you?" He gets his first good look
at her in the theater lights which just came on.
"How would you like to discuss Goddard
over a cup of cappuccino?" he responds,
hardly believing his assertive voice.
"Great! I've got nothing else to do.
What's your name?" she asks walking up
the aisle, "I'm Sally." He follows, "Lalaki,
it signifies man in Filipino." On the escalator,
she turns to him, "And what signifies a woman
in Filipino?" He looks up, "Long flowing hair,
spicy eyes, nice hips, Donna Karan jeans,
Steve Madden shoes, a love for French film—
a real *Babae*. Just like you." She breaks
into a smile, "Good answer."

■ ■ ■

ANG TUNAY NA LALAKI
MOVES INTO SALLY'S APARTMENT

on 5th Street between Avenue's B and C.
His plaid boxer shorts are already neatly tucked
in the bedroom drawers, shirts hanging
in the walk-in closet, most of his books on her shelves,
lap-top in a corner of the living room, and his toothbrush
and shaving supplies sharing her medicine cabinet.

There are three large railroad-type rooms
which can accommodate two sofas each, lots of wall space
for his posters of the Banaue rice terraces,
the chocolate hills of Bohol, the Mayon Volcano,
the sailing Vintas of Zamboanga, and of the old walled city
of Intramuros, Manila. The kitchen has a 50's dinette set
with a formica top, a full-range oven which had already been
baptized with the pungent spills of his Filipino cooking.

It was after he had cooked his sixth dinner
for Sally when he slipped the diamond engagement ring
into her halo-halo (a desert with shaved ice, filled
with tropical fruit, sweet cassava, and milk and sugar).
"I hope you haven't made this special halo-halo
for every woman you've met," she said, slipping
the ring on her finger. "It fits! When can you move in?"

■ ■ ■
SALLY'S RESUME

EDUCATION: Master of Arts, Film and Video Production, 1990
New York University, New York, NY

Bachelor of Arts, Literature and Languages, 1988
Bennington College, Bennington, VT

Clark High School, San Antonio, TX, 1984

EXPERIENCE: WNET, New Jersey, 1996-present.
    -Camera Operator, Stationary and Hand-held
    -Assistant to the Set Manager
The Ricky Lake Show, New York, 1995-1996
    -Assistant to the Producer
    -Researcher

The New School for Social Research, New York, 1992-95
    -Adjunct Faculty, Department of Humanities: Film
    -Courses taught: Undergraduate
      -Video Production, Editing
      -The Fundamentals of Sound and Lighting
      -Introduction to Film

AWARDS: National Endowment for the Arts Fellowship, 1993 for the
Documentary: *The Circular Life of the Foreskin*, 1992

Toronto Film Festival, Director's Prize, 1992
in the Experimental Film Category: *The Circular Life of
the Foreskin*

Miami Film Festival, Special Mention, 1991
for short video/film: *Vulva as Bible*

RESIDENCIES: The MacDowell Colony, summer 1990, winter 1994
Virginia Center for the Creative Arts, summer 1992
Villa Montalvo, summer 1991

SPECIAL
SKILLS   -Fluent in French, Spanish, American Sign Language
-Types 60 words per minute
-Problem solving, delivering ahead of deadline, team
  leader

REFERENCES: Upon request

■ ■ ■

ANG TUNAY NA LALAKI
LIES ON THE COUCH WATCHING TV

all day and Sally suggests he find
a hobby—anything to get him out of the apartment.
She hands him a flyer, "Honey, I passed by
the Asian American Writer's Workshop
at 37 St. Mark's Place and they have these poetry
classes you can take. Those love poems you wrote me
were pretty good." He leans over to kiss,
keeping one eye on Captain Janeway who's just given
the order to fire photon torpedoes from the Starship
Voyager, "Sure Sweetie. Love poems."
"Look, Honey, the workshop starts tomorrow," she says,
placing the flyer between his line of sight and the TV,
"I paid and registered for you already and Nick Carbó
will be your teacher." He forgets Star Trek,
stares at the piece of paper, "A few months ago I met
a nut case who said he knew this poet guy."

She slips her arms around his neck, "Will you
write me more love poems? About my being
the air you breathe, your souffle, your cello,
your musical merry-go-round horse?"
She mounts his lap, begins a scintillatingly slow
up and down ride. Ang Tunay na Lalaki reaches
under her skirt, inches her purple panties down.

ANG TUNAY NA LALAKI
MEETS THE POET

in front of 37 St. Mark's Place smoking a cigarette.
"Can I have a stick for a quarter?" he asks Nick.
"If you're here for the poetry workshop,"
Nick responds, "It's free." Ang Tunay na Lalaki
inhales deeply, "Hey, American Spirit! My brand too.
You must work here, is this Carbó guy any good?"
Nick exhales, "I've taken a few of his workshops
and he's wild, man. He does weird writing exercises
that get you thinking dangerous stuff. You'll like it."
Ang Tunay na Lalaki studies Nick's round face,
"What, he inspires people to act on their urges
to violently overthrow the government? You
look familiar. Are you Filipino?" Nick smiles,
"Poetry *can* make things happen! Yes, from Manila."
Ang Tunay na Lalaki scrutinizes the poet's shoes,
"States-side *ka na? Taga saan, sa Maynila?*"
"*May* green card *na ako.* Sa Makati. I went
to the International School," responds Nick.
Ang Tunay na Lalaki puts out his cigarette,
"*Siguro* big shot *ang pamilya mo. Anong*
pangalan mo, pare?" Nick stomps out his cigarette,
"No, no big shots in our family. And I'm Nick Carbó.
Time to go down stairs and start the workshop."
Ang Tunay na Lalaki follows, "No shit! *Pare?*
You're a real person! There's a Greek guy
running around the city who calls himself Orpheus
saying he's a character from one of your poems.
It's true, I met him and he tried to pick me up."
Nick holds the black door open, "It's the Republicans.
They closed all the mental wards and released
thousands of nut cases into the streets. Now, that's scary."

■ ■ ■
ANG TUNAY NA LALAKI'S
FIRST WORKSHOP POEM

Reflections

I've always been afraid of mirrors—
of the infinity

of selves the shiny ~~surfuce~~ surface
can produce,

of the universe
that may lie beyond the smallest

reflection inside the mirror.
Does the reflected image telescope

out into some other side
getting bigger,

to reach the other me?
I've always been afraid that the other

me would be no different,
that we

would be leading exactly
the same lives.

■ ■ ■
ANG TUNAY NA LALAKI'S
SECOND WORKSHOP POEM

Red

A woman with a red
parasol walks
up Spring Street.

She belongs
more to the red parasol
than any woman

in the city.
It's not
the red socks

around her ankles,
nor the red horn-rimmed
sunglasses

that makes the match
so perfect.
It's the smile

in her step
and the red shadow
following

along the hot
concrete
sidewalk.

■ ■ ■
ANG TUNAY NA LALAKI'S
THIRD WORKSHOP POEM

Seduction 1

~~Her name is Sally.~~
~~She nibbles my buttons.~~
~~She loves the string's flavor~~

~~Sally has black hair but is really blond.~~
~~She wants to dye my black pubic hair blond~~
~~to match hers when we make love.~~

Sally walks with black hair
but is really a blond. She wants to dye
my black crotch hairs blond to match hers
when we make love in the dark.

Sally sits naked on the edge of the tub
shaking the bottle of Clairol Nice N Easy
as I stand before her with my boxer shorts
kicked to the side. I run my hands

from her face to her shiny ~~silky~~ black hair,
making it cascade over her white shoulders.
Sally puts on the plastic gloves, surveys
the area with pure clinical detail.

I am surprised that I don't get an erection,
just a rolling of the sack. Sally slowly applies
the dye, she says it might sting a little.
She rubs it in even over the balls.

Sally says we have to wait twenty minutes
so I sit next to her on the tub and french kiss
her ~~sweet~~ lickable lips. That's when I get
a hard-on, a woody, a boner, a thirty-story rise.

Twenty minutes and Sally places me in the tub,
washes away the dark dye with warm water.
She removes her plastic gloves, enters the tub,
inspects the hairs with her lips, swallows me whole.

■ ■ ■
ANG TUNAY NA LALAKI'S
FOURTH WORKSHOP POEM

Aswang vs Wonder Woman

From the ~~Wonder~~ invisible plane
Wonder Woman spots
~~a giant~~ big black bat wings flitting

from window to window
along the upper west side
of Manhattan. This could be

the monster that's been sucking
live fetuses from pregnant mothers.
Wonder Woman dives

for a closer look, notices
~~it's just~~ it has a torso and two arms,
and a woman's head with long

black hair. She's eating something
fleshy and raw! Wonder Woman
gets on the radio, calls

the Justice League for back up.
It's too late, the Aswang is breaking
the glass of her cockpit. Aqua Man

answers, "Sending the Green Lantern
and Hawk Man. Over." The Aswang
has reached in, grabbed

the receiver from her hand
and its bloody ~~dog~~ canine teeth
ripping into Wonder Woman's

Wonder bracelet. She pushes the eject
button, catapults into the sky
to escape the ~~sharp~~ smelly Aswang teeth.

But Wonder Woman is not
out of it yet—the *Aswang* has
good radar, finds Wonder Woman

as she's falling, grabs
her by the legs and bites
into the golden boots.

Wonder Woman screams, "Let go!
You immigrant scum!" The *Aswang*
extends its claws,

"*Putang ina mo!* Yankee go
home!" Wonder Woman receives
gashes through her red, white,

and blue toga, "Speak English!
You foreign piece of crap! Ouch!"
The *Aswang* responds, "Eat my

bulbul you ugly American. And
have a nice trip!" letting go
of Wonder Woman's legs.

She is about to splat onto
Riverside Drive when a big fluffy
green baseball mitt appears

below her to break her fall.
"You're lucky I got here fast,"
Green Lantern says,

"And boy, you sure look
beat up." Wonder Woman searches
the sky, "When I get my

golden lasso around the neck
of that Filipino bitch monster,
I'll squeeze and never let go."

Hawk Man is in pursuit
of the *Aswang*, chasing it under
elevated subway trains,

around the Chrysler building,
past the glowing tower
of the Empire State building.

Wonder Woman nurses her wounds
as she watches two sets of wings disappear
into dots above the New York sky line.

■ ■ ■
ANG TUNAY NA LALAKI'S
FIFTH WORKSHOP POEM

Light Years

In the photographic print
Constellation of Opposites, 1996
by Barbara Ess,
the whole background is black,
small buoyant white dots appear
not quite in orderly staggered rows
across the deep surface.
They look like stars,
they seem to twinkle as you walk
from left to right and right to left.
When you enter an inner orbit,
passing inches from the print,
you see the stars are human faces
reduced to diminutive dots
that allude to distance.

The most distant object
ever seen from earth is a young
galaxy: Red Arc in CL1358+62
measured at 13 billion light years
from our planet. I suspect
the expressions on those Ess faces
have traveled a long way
for billions and billions of years
wearing those maniacal smiles
after our universe was born,
after the big bang.

■ ■ ■

ANG TUNAY NA LALAKI
RECEIVES INSTRUCTIONS FOR HIS
LAST WORKSHOP POEM

You will need a pen and a piece of paper.

1

You will go up the stairs into St. Mark's Place,
go up to a stranger and ask him/her to give you one word.
Example: "Hi, I'm writing a poem and I was wondering
if you could spare a word, any word that comes to mind."
(Don't forget to thank the stranger.)
You will write that word down as number 1.

2

You will walk up to the intersection of Lafayette
and St. Mark's (Astor Place). You will stand
next to the giant cube metal sculpture on the middle
traffic island and you will listen
for a specific sound—an onomatopoetic sound.
Example: Grrrrr-ting, grrrrrrrrrrr-ting, grrrrrrrrrr
of a jack hammer pounding on asphalt.
(Stand there at least ten minutes, filter out
the first three obvious sounds. Listen
for the subtle sounds of a plastic bag blowing by,
the wheels of a baby stroller, the scrape
of a leather shoe made in Italy.)
You will write that sound down as number 2.

3

You will walk to the Barnes & Noble book store
on Broadway and St. Mark's. You will enter
the store and go up the escalator or elevator or stairs
to the second floor Poetry Section. You will choose

a book of poems from the many shelves.
You will open the book to the second poem
and you will read the first line of that poem.
You will write down that line.
(Don't forget to put the book back after
you note the author of the poem and the title.)
You will write that line down as number 3.

4

You will walk back to the Astor Place subway
entrance (the uptown side). You will go down
the stairs and stand near the exit turnstiles.
You will look for the expression on the face
of the first person to exit from the train.
Example: Gruff, solemn, elated, kind, needy.
(No need to interact with individual.)
You will write that expression down as number 4.

5

You will walk back to the workshop at 37 St. Mark's Place.
Along the way, you will catch the momentary scent
of something in the air. You will look for
and identify the source of the scent.
Example: Pizza, bus exhaust, a woman's perfume,
urine on the sidewalk, rotting garbage.
(Don't frighten the female pedestrians by trying
to smell their hair as they walk by.)
You will write the scent down as number 5.

6

You will come back to this table and decide
whether to begin writing the poem for the remainder
of the class time or go home to write it over the weekend.

You will write a poem with six stanzas,
each stanza will have six lines of varying lengths.
In the first stanza you will begin the poem with the word
in #1, you will also use that word in the sixth stanza.
In the second stanza you will incorporate
the sound, #2, in any of the six lines.
In the third stanza you will use
the first line from the book, #3, for the last line
of the stanza and the last lines in each of the six stanzas.
In the fourth stanza you will place the expression
of that face, #4, in any of the six lines.
In the fifth stanza you will put the scent,
#5, in any of the six lines.
In the sixth stanza you will use the word in #1
anywhere in lines 2 and 4.
(Good luck.)

■ *for Fiona Templeton*

■ ■ ■
SALLY SPEAKS

You're damn right I'm your anima!
Count them. You've given me
only 31 lines so far and my appearance
is described through the eyes
of Lalaki and through a paltry resumé.
You've even given my mother
a clearer voice—she gets
a whole poem to herself, and what?
This is supposed to establish
a complex psychological history
between a mother and daughter?

Picture the reviewers out there
saying, "The main Filipino character
is depicted in poignant and hysterical
adventures which inform us about
the complex psyche of a recent immigrant's
postcolonial experience of attempting
to survive in the *motherland*. However,
the girlfriend-turned-wife is left
as a stick-figure with a nebulous past
and an insipid personality."

I'm not a spoiled actress demanding more lines.
I just don't understand my motivation!

O.K. I admit it. I love him but this
came out of nowhere—and I'm supposed
to marry him now? What happened
to the dozens of roses, the long walks
through Central Park, the candle-lit dinners,
the weekend trips to Montauk?

A woman should be romanced first
before the future mother-in-law comes
into the picture making potato pancakes.

This is your first warning,
and remember, you need me.

Part
Four
...

ANG TUNAY NA LALAKI
CONSIDERS THE HISTORICAL CONSEQUENCES

of his marriage to a [white] American woman
and the immediate thought he gets is that they would be
legally practicing inter-racial sex. Savagely good
cafe con leche sex with rain forest honey to sweeten
the taste. Hah! those early anti-miscegenation laws
could not prevent brown and white pheromones
from intertwining in the dance halls and bedrooms
of Stockton, Petaluma, Santa Barbara, Napa Valley.

"It is a dreadful thing when these Filipinos,
scarcely more than savages, come to San Francisco,
work for practically nothing, and obtain
the society of these [white] girls. . . .
Some of these [Filipino] boys, with perfect candor,
have told me bluntly and boastfully
that they practice the art of love with more perfection
than white boys, and occasionally one of the [white] girls
has supplied me with information to the same effect.
In fact some of the disclosures in this regard
are perfectly startling in nature."
    —San Francisco Municipal Court Judge Sylvain Lazarus,
        in *Time*, vol. 28 (April 13, 1936), p.17.

Is that why they came up with the myth
of the pin-size Asian penis? Think about it—
a frank discussion in the mid 1930's by an American judge
in a nationally distributed magazine about the sexual
prowess of Filipino males. A *little* threat perhaps?

"We Filipinos, however poor, are taught
from the cradle up to respect and love our women.

That's why our divorce rate is nil compared
with the State of which Judge Lazarus is a proud son.
If to respect and love womenfolks is savagery,
then make the most of it, Judge. We plead guilty."
    —Ernest Ilustre, in a letter to the editor
    in *Time*, vol. 28 (April 27, 1936), p. 6.

■ ■ ■

ANG TUNAY NA LALAKI
LIES NUDE ON THE BED

with klieg lights illuminating his brown muscles.
His body is the subject of Sally's new 16mm film—

20 minutes—brown nipple
20 minutes—brown butt cheeks
20 minutes—brown knee
20 minutes—brown penis—

he feels odd being the object of desire.

Sally splices the footage of his body
with images of American soldiers posing
during the Philippine-American War of 1899-1902.
She asks him to urinate on the strips of negative.
She asks him to masturbate with baby oil
twenty times and ejaculate on the negatives.
She records the sounds of his hand on his penis
to use in a loop as the sound-track for the film.
She projects the crusty but textured film on the wall,
asks him to pose nude in front of the image
and produce several cowering poses,
pretending the projector is a Krag-Jorgensen rifle.
She shoots 30 more minutes of this scene
with the earlier images playing over his brown body
and around the white background.
She also projects the texts of racist songs
sung by the American soldiers:

Damn, damn, damn the Filipinos!
Cut-throat khakiac ladrones!
Underneath the starry flag,

Civilize them with a Krag,
And return us to our beloved home.

and

They say I've got brown brothers here,
But still I draw the line.
He may be a brother of Big Bill Taft,
But he ain't no brother of mine.

Sally edits the film down to 28 minutes,
she titles it Pissing On Our Past
and it wins a funding grant
from the National Endowment for the Arts.

■ ■ ■
POLYSOMNOGRAPHY
INTERPRETATION REPORT

Patient: Lalaki, Ang Tunay na
PSG#: 518-1
MR#: 308315
Lights Out: 2316
Lights on: 0603
HT: 68in   WT: 197 lbs   AGE: 31/Male

COMMENTS: R/O Sleep Apnea Syndrome.
MEDICATION: None.

SLEEP ARCHITECTURE:

The total recording
time
was 406.5 minutes.
The patient slept
for 231.5 minutes, with a sleep
efficiency
of 56.9%. The
sleep latency
was 47 minutes, and
latency to REM
sleep
was 208.5 minutes.
The patient had
a total of 31.3% Stage
1 sleep, 46.2% Stage
2 sleep, 18.1% Stage
3/4 sleep, and 4.3%
REM sleep. No
evidence

of seizure activity
observed.

RESPIRATION

Pri (or) to CPAP
treatment, there were 5
obstructive apneas, 9
obstructive hypopneas, 4
central apneas, and 14
central hypopneas seen
during the study,
which lasted up
to 20 seconds.
Mean
respiratory event
length was 14 seconds.
The total apnea/hypopnea
index (AHI) was 13.3
events per hour
of sleep.
Periods
of moderate snoring
were noted. Obstructive
breathing pattern observed
both in NREM
and REM sleep.

Due to
the number of respiratory
events and oxygen
desa-
turations, nasal
CPAP was tit-
rated starting at
4cm H2O pressure. The

apneas,
hypopneas,
oxygen desaturations,
and snoring
were eliminated
with nasal CPAP
at 8cm H2O pressure.

OXYGEN SATURATION

Oxygen sat (u) ration
varied from 97% baseline
while awake to a
low of 79%. There
were a total
of 10 desturations ass-
ociated with respiratory
events. After
CPAP treatment, the
patient's saturation stab-
ilized and stay (ed) above 90%.

ELECTROCARDIOGRAM:

Me (an) heart
rate was 89 bpm
during the study. No car-
diac arrhythmias
were noted.

ANTERIOR TIBIALIS EMG:

No (e) (v) (i) (d) (e) (n) (c) (e)
for Per-
io-
dic Limb M-

ovem-
ent Sy-
ndro-
me
was
se
en.

OBSERVATIONS:

1. Moderate obstructive sleep apnea.
2. Moderate snoring.

RECOMMENDATIONS:

1. Home use of nasal CPAP at 8cm H2O with sleep.
2. Weight reduction.

Nick Carbo, MFA
Interpreting Poet
Mt. Lazarus Sleep Disorders Center

RE: Lalaki, Ang Tunay na
PSG Report 518-1 Lalaki.doc

■ ■ ■
ANG TUNAY NA LALAKI
LOOKS AT THE EARLY AMERICANS

who sailed into Manila before 1898.
In 1786, the Continental Congress met
in Philadelphia and debated how
to urge Spain to grant the United States
trading privileges in Manila. Wiley
New England sea captains had already been
stopping at that port while plying
the orient seas with American mercantile.
One such sea captain was Nathaniel Bowditch
born in Salem, Massachusetts sailing
the *Astrea* on a scheduled port of call
in October 1796. The young (23 years) Captain
spent close to three months in Manila.
Some semblance of civilization
must have kept him occupied during
those long hot humid days. The Indio natives
weren't all savages swinging in trees
as they would be portrayed in the next century
during the Philippine American War.
"Captain Bowditch, would you like coffee,
tea, or brandy before we head off
to the Zarzuela? The Manileños come
in the latest European fashions, so please
dress accordingly. Afterwards,
the gentlemen may retire to a tavern
for more lively pursuits with the company
of precious Filipina *meztizas*. All those months
at sea, especially for such a virile Captain
as yourself, must take its toll
on your constitution." This is what
John Stuart Kerr, an American entrepreneur

already residing in Manila, must have said
to welcome his compatriot. Thus, was born
the unending cycle of prostitution to service
Americans which reached its height
with 50,000 precious Filipina prostitutes
in the late 20th century around the American
military and navy bases at Clark and Subic.

■ ■ ■
ANG TUNAY NA LALAKI
WRITES HIS DREAM DICTIONARY

"When you dream of jello, you dream of sorrow."
—Richard McCann

Feet: You are walking away from a situation.
                 Avoidance, evasion, deceit, run-around.

Hair: You are hungry for knowledge. Falling
                 hair: You are seeking a memory but can't
                 reach it. Long wet hair: You will find
                 the information you seek.

Eyes: You will drown in the water while
                 attempting to embrace the reflection
                 of the fullest moon. Passion.

Baby Corn: You desire the company of small people.

Galaxies: You are falling in love. A galaxy churning
                 then splitting apart: You are falling
                 out of love.

Urine: You will receive more rejected poems
                 in the mail. Also bad news about the grant,
                 fellowship, job application.

Parasol: You need to lose weight. No more Swiss
                 chocolates, whole milk, midnight Chinese
                 noodles, croissants, lobsters dripping
                 with butter, Spaghetti bolonghese.

The Statue
of Liberty: You will murder the Orpheus in you.
You will enjoy it.
You will cut his body into small chunks.
You will dispose of those chunks throughout
the subway tunnels of New York piece by piece.
You will throw his head over
the Brooklyn Bridge in honor of Hart Crane.

Cappuccino: You dream of Omphale the masculine
but attractive Queen of Lydia who enslaved
Hercules for three years which made him fall
in love with her. Hercules was made to live
an effeminate life, spinning wool, catering
to Omphale's every whim, while she wore
the lion's skin riding Hercules from atop.

Penis
extender: You have been deprived of early childhood
breast feeding by your mother. The bond
was broken too soon. A constant need
for an embrace.

Cigarette
smoke: Optimism. You dream of Leibnitz
who said, "whatever is, is right."

Purple: Caution. You should boil all water
for ten minutes to kill bacteria
before drinking.

Subway: You desire sexual intercourse.

Boxer
shorts: You dream of nostalgia.

Mangoes: You dream of sleep. A sleep
like that of the Greek poet
Epimenides who fell asleep
in a cave when he was a young
boy and woke up fifty-seven years
later having acquired all
the wisdom in the world.

Wonder
Woman: You desire unattainable buxom women.

Mirrors: You dream of having children.

Aswang: A demimonde. You dream of being
divided between two worlds, two
cultures, two minds.

■ ■ ■

ANG TUNAY NA LALAKI
TRIES TO EXPLAIN TO HIS THERAPIST

why he always feels so angry. "Did you know
that Filipino workers were once classified below
fertilizer in a list of farming supplies requisitioned
by an American landowner? No, that's not why
I'm angry. Let's begin with James Fenimore Cooper
and *The Last of the Mohicans*. Most of the Native
Americans were decimated throughout New England
by 1826 and Cooper, having been influenced
by the *noble savage* from Francois Rene de Chateaubriand's
novels, brings to his American contemporaries
an idealized, romantic view of the *Indians*. This
did not help prevent the massacre at Wounded Knee,
the Trail of Tears, the Apache Campaigns, the hounding
of the Nez Perce, the capture of Geronimo, and on
and on and on and on. Let's go to Harriet Beecher Stowe's
novel *Uncle Tom's Cabin*. In 1851 that book did well
in fanning the flames of anti-slavery and your nation
had to take arms against itself in the Civil War
to abolish a festering evil. So, Lincoln freed the slaves.
All this while operating under a Constitution whose
first ideals are *All men are created equal*. And
it was not until a hundred years later that they added
the 13th and 14th Amendments to the Constitution
granting Civil Rights to the grandchildren, great-
grandchildren of those freed black slaves. Meanwhile,
in 1898, the United States, itself a former colony
having cast its shackles from its master, becomes
an empire by taking Cuba, Puerto Rico, and
the Philippines from Spain. To the eyes of the world,
you had become a conquering race, conquistadors
with Manifest Destiny, Progress, Democracy

as your swords. No American has dared admit,
that they are a conquering people unless they
were willing to be caught in a hypocritical lie.
All your sins seem to be erased from memory,
given scant mention in text books:
the Chinese Exclusion Act, the internment
of the Japanese during the Second World War, the rape
of Mexico in the mid 1800's, the fact that
Puerto Rico is still, in essence, an American colony,
the persecution of suspected communists under
Senator McCarthy, the invasion of Santo Domingo,
the deposing of South American Presidents.
The silence of serial murderers never lasts long,
somehow they want to be stopped, they want
to be caught. They are proud of their sinister deeds."

■ *for Raquel Ortiz*

Part
Five

...

■ ■ ■
SECRET ASIAN MAN

He's given a number,
he's given a new name,
he's given an automatic pistol,
he's given a license to kill.

He could be Chinese, Nepalese,
Cambodian, Timorese, Laotian,
Indonesian, Burmese, or Thai.

He can kick higher than Jackie Chan,
he can be as devious as Dr. Fu Manchu,
he can speak better English than Charlie Chan,
and he can even make a great pot of Moo Goo Gai Pan.

He could be Korean, Japanese,
Singaporean, Malaysian, Tibetan,
Vietnamese, or from Brunei.

He'll torture you with drops of water between the eyes,
shove bamboo strips under your nails and dip them in iodine.
He'll torture you by tying you up in a wicker chair,
make you watch endless reruns of Kung Fu with David Carradine.

He's given a number,
he's given a new name,
he's given an automatic pistol,
he's given a license to kill.

■ ■ ■
ASSIGNMENT

His first job is to guard the Hello Kitty character from Sanrio Toys. She's on her New York leg of a world tour and right away the paparazzi have her centered in their camera lenses. Rumors say she's in love with Barney the purple dinosaur—a Japanese and American, pink and purple inter-racial romance—something out of the pages of the novel Shogun or from the opera *Madame Butterfly*.

Barney has all the power, has the 60% US market share Hello Kitty needs to warm her way into the hearts of pre-K American boys and girls.

The Secret Asian Man holds back the screaming little fans of Hello Kitty as she emerges from the Soho Grand Hotel on West Broadway. Hundreds of bulbs flash as Barney helps her step into the pink limo. Suddenly, from out of the crowd, a tall man in a Power Rangers suit jumps up to the driver's side, punches the driver out cold, pulls him out of the car, and climbs in to screech away burning rubber.

Hello Kitty screams "Help me! Help me! I'm being kidnapped!" from the window.

The Secret Asian Man looks around, notices Barney hysterically jumping up and down, mumbling "I love her! I love Kitty! Catch them!"

All the children are crying and he realizes this is real, this is not a stunt dreamed up by the toy companies. The Secret Asian Man commandeers a Honda motorcycle from a passing citizen and gives chase to the pink limo. He reaches West Broadway & Canal, spots the car speeding through Chinatown. He's right behind them now but the limo swerves onto the sidewalk smashing into carts of exotic comestibles. Whole roasted Peking ducks are flying everywhere—fresh lychee fruit, bitter melon, dried tiny shrimp, bean sprouts, giant jack fruit, coconuts, and steamed pork buns fall in his path but he skillfully avoids them all.

The Secret Asian Man thinks "That Hong Kong movie director John Woo would love the way I'm dodging all these obstacles." The pink limo swerves back into the street and slams its brakes in front of a passing fish truck. The Secret Asian Man is going too fast and he crashes into the back of the pink limo—the impact sending him flying over the car and into the truck with the sign, LIVE MAINE CRABS.

With his way blocked by the truck, the Power Ranger pulls Hello Kitty out from the pink limo and drags her along Mott Street. The Secret Asian Man climbs out of the water tank inside the truck as large crabs cling to his clothes with their stubborn claws. A group of German tourists point at and take pictures of "das krab man!"

He catches a glimpse of Hello Kitty's red ribbon bobbing in the middle of the shopping crowd and he runs after them. He gets within five feet of the target near Mott & Grand, pulls out his automatic pistol and shouts "freeze!" (a phrase he remembers Jack Lord saying in his favorite TV show as a kid growing up in the 70's, *Hawaii Five-O*).

The Power Ranger shoves Hello Kitty toward the Secret Asian Man and in that moment of distraction, kicks the gun out of his hands and turns to deliver a round house kick to the head with his other foot. The Secret Asian Man is stunned and he realizes that this is not one of the re-done American Power Rangers played by American teenagers. This guy is an original player and dangerous!

From out of the gathering crowd, Hello Kitty runs up and pounces on the leg of the Power Ranger, clawing his calf. This gives the Secret Asian Man enough time to launch a high kick to the Power Ranger's head and knock him senseless into the ground. The crowd of shoppers clap as if they had just watched a scene from an action movie and the good guy had just won. The Secret Asian Man bows, takes his shiny handcuffs, places them on the kidnapper's wrists.

■ ■ ■
CAUGHT

Sally sits on a bench in Central Park reading the *New York Times Sunday Magazine*. Across the lawn is Tavern on the Green restaurant with expensively dressed people coming in and out for lunch. She takes a sip from her Diet Coke and spots a guy who looks so much like Ang Tunay na Lalaki that she blows the diet coke back down the straw into the bottle.

A tall, leggy brunette with bright orange platform shoes, short turquoise skirt, and matching bright orange blouse is hanging onto his arm as if she knew the color and texture of his boxer shorts. Sally thinks—*If that's my fiance, I'm going to stuff that woman's orange shoes down his throat.*

Sally pops up for a closer look, her mind racing—*he doesn't even own a black Armani suit but that swagger in his walk is unmistakable.Could it be him? They both have on matching pairs of killer sunglasses.* Sally speeds up to intercept the couple from behind. As she passes,
she picks out the scent of Hugo Boss, his favorite cologne.

Sally is about to turn around and scream *You asshole!* when Lalaki's voice blurts out from behind. "Hey, that's my fiance. Honey, what are you doing here?"

Now she has to face them, wipe the anger from her lips and present a cheery, *Hi, fancy running into you in Central Park!*

The tall woman has stopped clinging to his arm and Lalaki says, "Sally, this is Tatiana from Budapest. We work together at the agency and we're partners on some cases."

Sally offers a hand and a half-moon smile.

"So, nice, to, meet, you, Miss, Budapest."

Lalaki corrects her, "No, she's a model from Budapest, a city in Hungary, and her name is Tatiana."

Sally can only hear the car horns blowing on 5th Avenue. The sky is turquoise with a few clouds, people are jogging, and she focuses on a mole on Tatiana's long neck. There is an awkward silence until Sally blurts out, "There's my bus downtown. Gotta go!" She runs off to the distant street corner, hops up the stairs, and fumbles for a token in her purse as the bus pulls away.

■ ■ ■
FIGHT

"What do you fucking mean it's part of your job?" Sally has torn down all of Lalaki's Filipino posters, burned them in the tub along with all of his clothes. The smell of smoke lingers in the apartment.

"We were meeting a Cuban diplomat who wants to defect. Everything I do is of national importance," responds Lalaki.

"Is humiliating me part of the job?" Sally asks, glaring at him and his silk Valentino tie.

"Budapest IS a city in eastern Europe, dear," responds Lalaki as he tries to reach for her hand.

Sally swats it away, "I know that! But I saw you carousing with that tall Slavic woman and what am I supposed to think? Say something, you incontinent worm!"

"No, I'm not having an affair with that *Hungarian* woman. On a few cases I am required to pretend to be married to other women as a cover. That's why I have different clothes, sometimes a different accent. There, I've divulged too much already. I'm a secret agent. It's a job!" responds Lalaki as he lights a cigarette.

"Do you also pretend to fuck them? Is that what you've been doing when you had to go away for those four to six day trips?" asks Sally, uncrossing her arms.

"No, that's so unfair of you to think that. It's against policy to boink your co-workers and we are usually assigned separate rooms in hotels. Those trips are boring—meetings all over the city, long periods of observation, debriefings, and so much paperwork," Lalaki answers making his way to their blue couch. Sally follows but sits on the other end.

"Then who are you really? An actor? A poet? A secret agent man?"

Lalaki puts out his cigarette, "Remember honey, you met the real me, the real man before I applied for this job. You'll always have the genuine article at home and for the rest of your life."

Sally allows him to kiss the palm of her hand, "Well, I won't ask you to quit your job but you have to do one thing for me. Take off all your clothes."

Lalaki removes his Valentino tie, his Armani jacket and matching pants, his Polo boxer shorts and hands it all to her. She smiles a small evil smile, brings the clothes to the charred bathtub, pours turpentine over the last of his garments and lights a match.

Sally runs a hand on Lalaki's chest and with the other, she squeezes his flaccid penis hard, "If I ever smell another woman on your body, I'll fry this first."

REVENGE

Lalaki returns from a six week-long trip to Europe and it seems nobody is home in the apartment. There is a fresh bouquet of red roses on the coffee table and a pair of black penny loafers by the blue couch. He catches muffled sounds coming from the bedroom. Gingerly, he removes his .33 caliber automatic pistol from his briefcase. With his back to the wall, he proceeds down the hall and jumps into a firing crouch with his pistol pointing into the darkness of the room.

He does not pull the trigger—Sally is in the throes of *Yes! Yes!* as a man thrusts between her thighs. *I can kill him with one bullet, he thinks, but that would be messy.* Lalaki puts down his gun—shock turning into jealousy, anger, the sting of betrayal.

Sally opens her eyes, sees Lalaki standing by the foot of the bed. There is a slight look of surprise but her gaze is strong, challenging him to do something. Lalaki starts to take off his clothes. Sally goes through another round of *Yes! Yes!* He walks to the head of the bed, approaching like a matador with his eyes focused on the *estocada*, the sword thrust into the bull's neck.

Sally silently reaches for Lalaki's swelling penis. The man thrusting between her legs looks up and calmly says, "I knew you'd come, my friend."

Lalaki recognizes him and it's Orpheus, the guy from the cafe on Mott Street.

He feels Sally's lips on his foreskin, her tongue swirling around the head. He closes his eyes, enjoying the familiar sensations. When he looks down again, Orpheus is now sucking his penis to the root.

Sally's hand is caressing his testicles and he thinks, *I can't believe this is happening. Is this real?*

He extricates his penis from the two pairs of lips, climbs on top of Orpheus who says, *Yes! Yes!* quickening his thrusts into Sally.

Lalaki slings his right forearm under Orpheus' neck and begins a secure chocking hold. He watches Sally's eyes as he tightens his grip. She is still challenging him with her silent look. He feels

Orpheus' back, shoulder, and thigh muscles struggling to free itself. All he manages is a series of violent forward thrusts into Sally.

Lalaki keeps the pressure for more than ten minutes. Sally finally breaks her silence, "I think you've made your point. He's dead. He came and he died."

■ ■ ■
EPILOGUE

At this point of the book
I feel compelled to abandon you,
my dear reader, as Paul Valery
would have me do. But first,
to be fair, I'd like to leave you
with an image that came as a dream:
Ang Tunay na Lalaki and Sally are standing
before a District Court Judge. He is dressed
in a tuxedo, she, in an off-the-shoulder white satin
and silk Vera Wang dress. Lalaki and Sally kiss.
She is three months pregnant. The bride
and groom's parents are there as witnesses
and each is proud of their child, this union.

As for me, I'll be on my way to the Harmony Palace
restaurant on Mott Street in thirty minutes
for the reception. My wife Denise has wrapped
the gift. We want to give them a good life.